WHAT SHOULD I DO? WHAT SHOULD I DO?

COMMUNITY · CONNECTIONS

WHAT SHOULD I DO?
ON THE PLAYGROUND

BY WIL MARA

CHERRY LAKE
Publishing

Published in the United States of America by Cherry Lake Publishing
Ann Arbor, Michigan
www.cherrylakepublishing.com

Content Adviser: Karen Sheehan, MD, MPH, Children's Memorial Hospital, Chicago, Illinois

Photo Credits: Cover and page 1, ©Denise Mondloch; page 5, ©Cheryl Casey/Shutterstock, Inc.; page 7, ©planet5D LLC/Shutterstock, Inc.; page 9, ©Monkey Business Images/Shutterstock, Inc.; page 11, ©vblinov/Shutterstock, Inc.; page 13, ©Marzanna Syncerz/Dreamstime.com; page 15, ©Steve Cukrov/Shutterstock, Inc.; page 17, ©majeczka/Shutterstock, Inc.; page 19, ©Teresa Kenney/Dreamstime.com; page 21, ©Ron Chapple Studios/Dreamstime.com

LIBRARY OF CONGRESS CATALOGING-IN-PUBLICATION DATA
Mara, Wil.
   What should I do? On the playground/by Wil Mara.
      p. cm.—(Community connections)
   Includes bibliographical references and index.
   ISBN-13: 978-1-61080-054-9 (lib. bdg.)
   ISBN-10: 1-61080-054-0 (lib. bdg.)
   1. Playgrounds—Safety measures—Juvenile literature. I. Title. II. Series.
   GV424.M37 2012
   790.06'8—dc22   2011000128

Cherry Lake Publishing would like to acknowledge the work of The Partnership for 21st Century Skills. Please visit www.21stcenturyskills.org for more information.

Printed in the United States of America
Corporate Graphics Inc.
July 2011
CLFA09

ON THE PLAYGROUND

CONTENTS

WHAT SHOULD I DO?

FUN BUT DANGEROUS

A playground is a fun place. There is so much to do there. But a playground can also be **dangerous**. You can get hurt if you do not follow some safety rules. Do you know what those rules are?

Be careful while you are having fun on the playground.

THINK!

Take a good
look around the
playground. Do you
see any ways that
someone could get
hurt? What are they?
What can you do to
avoid getting hurt?

IT IS EASY
TO GET HURT

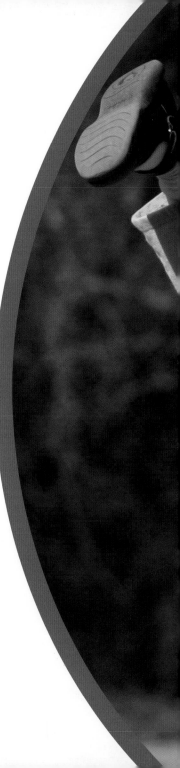

Playgrounds have many things
to play on. You can climb up
high or spin around very fast.
Other children will often be on
the playground, too.

It is very easy to fall down
or run into something. You could
cut yourself or even break a bone.

If you do not sit right on a swing, you
could fall off.

Look at your clothes before you go to a playground. Make sure they are not too loose. Loose clothes can get caught on things. Also make sure there are no strings hanging anywhere. Tie your hair back if it is long.

PLAYGROUND SAFETY RULES

Always make sure an adult is watching you. Your parents or a very close family friend would be good choices. They will be able to help you if you get hurt. They can also watch out for **strangers**.

An adult can help you stay safe during a visit to the playground.

Make sure you always use playground **equipment** the right way. Do not try to run down a slide. Always slide down it the way you are supposed to.

Most children get hurt on playgrounds by fooling around. They also get hurt when trying to show off for their friends.

Come down a slide feet first to play it safe.

Play nicely with other children at the playground. Make sure you share the equipment. Do not try to hog everything or always be first in line.

Everyone will have fun if they use good **behavior**. Do not play near children who aren't behaving. Tell an adult about them.

If everyone plays nicely together, everyone will have fun.

Do not use playground equipment that is in bad condition. Avoid **rusty** equipment. Stay away from equipment that has loose or broken parts. Watch out for sharp edges and **pinch spots**. Be careful around old wooden equipment. It can give you splinters.

It would not be safe to play on this old swing!

15

The safest playgrounds have soft **surfacing** on the ground. The best kinds of surfacing are wood chips, pea gravel, and tiny bits of rubber. Rubber mats are also good. Avoid playgrounds that have hard surfacing such as dirt or concrete. You will fall sooner or later. You do not want to fall on anything hard.

Surfaces such as the rubber mats on this playground help keep you safe.

You should always check to make sure there is no trash or other junk lying around. Be careful of things such as broken glass, nails, and rocks. Also avoid playgrounds that are slippery because of rain, snow, or ice.

Empty soda cans and other trash make playgrounds unsafe.

Make a list of all the playgrounds near your home. Then ask your parents to bring you to each one so you can look for dangers. Cross the most dangerous playgrounds off the list. Only go back to the safe playgrounds.

IF YOU DO GET HURT

There are times when you will get hurt on a playground. Bumps and scratches are a normal part of being a kid! Make sure you tell an adult when this happens. Do not try to treat any scratches or cuts by yourself.

Playgrounds can be dangerous. But they are also a lot of fun when you follow the rules!

Ask an adult you know for help if you get hurt on the playground.

What should you do as soon as you get home from a playground? Wash your hands! It doesn't matter how clean a playground might seem. You will still get dirty. You might even need a bath or a shower if you get extra dirty.

GLOSSARY

behavior (bee-HAYV-yuhr) the way someone acts

dangerous (DAYN-jur-us) potentially harmful

equipment (ee-KWIP-ment) playground items such as slides, swings, or jungle gyms

pinch spots (PINCH SPOTS) parts of playground equipment that can catch your skin and pinch you

rusty (RUST-ee) the crusty, brownish coating that forms on many types of metal

strangers (STRAYN-jurz) people you do not know

surfacing (SUR-fiss-ing) any material that covers the ground for safety

FIND OUT MORE

BOOKS

Cuyler, Margery. *Please Play Safe! Penguin's Guide to Playground Safety*. New York: Scholastic, 2006.

Donahue, Jill Urban. *Play It Smart: Playground Safety*. Minneapolis: Picture Window Books, 2009.

Knowlton, Marylee. *Safety at the Playground*. New York: Crabtree Publishing, 2009.

WEB SITES

AAOS—Playground Safety: Tips for Kids
orthoinfo.aaos.org/topic.cfm?topic=A00345
Read about the best ways to avoid hurting yourself at the playground.

KidsHealth—Playgrounds
kidshealth.org/kid/stay_healthy/fit/playground.html
Read some safety tips for using different kinds of playground equipment.

INDEX

ABOUT THE AUTHOR

Wil Mara is the award-winning author of more than 120 books, many of which are educational titles for children. More information about his work can be found at *www.wilmara.com*.